There be **treasure** inside these here **pages!**

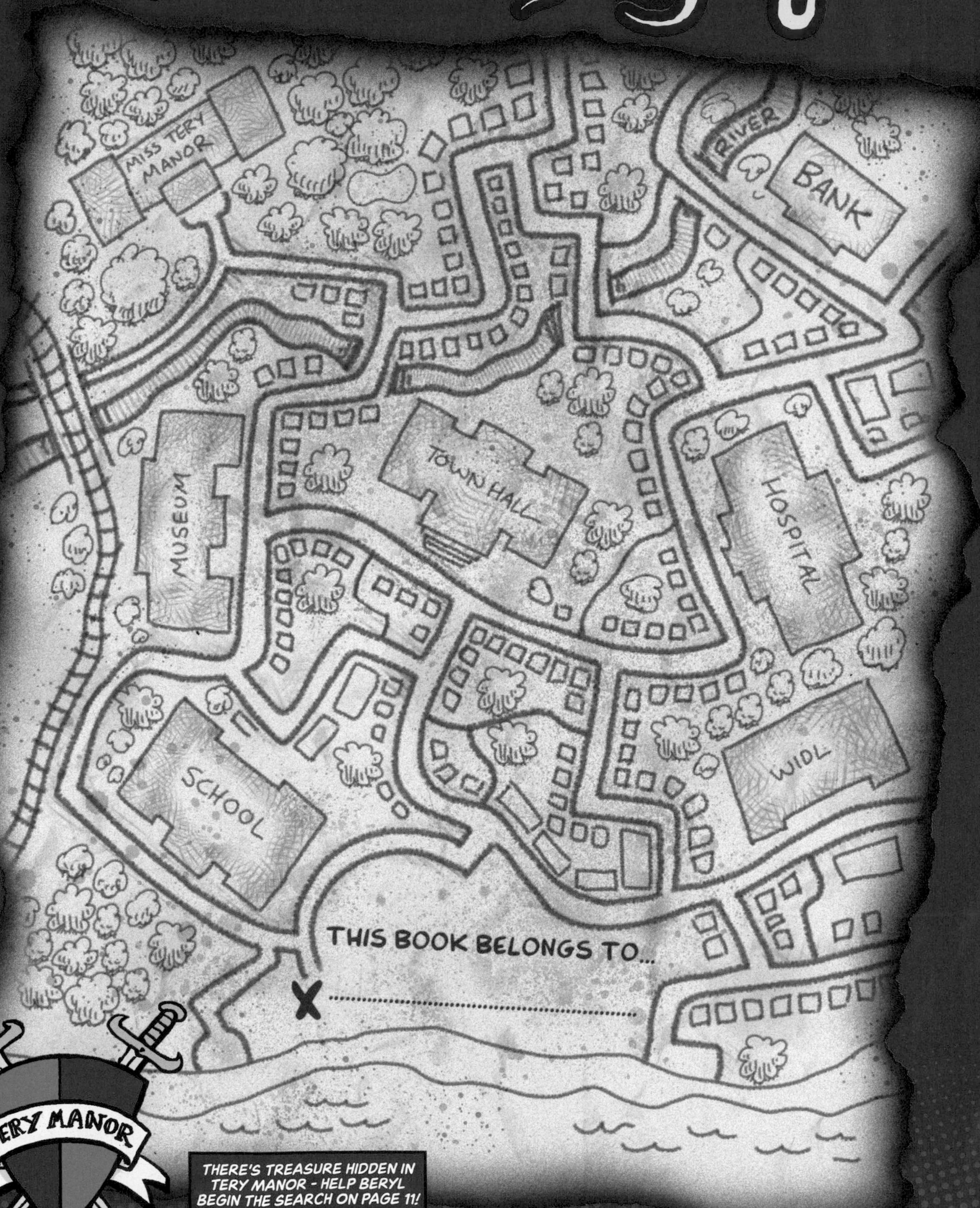

THE Dandy

MISS TERY MANOR

RIVER

BANK

MUSEUM

TOWN HALL

HOSPITAL

SCHOOL

WIDL

THIS BOOK BELONGS TO...

X ....

TERY MANOR

THERE'S TREASURE HIDDEN IN TERY MANOR - HELP BERYL BEGIN THE SEARCH ON PAGE 11!

the JOCKS and the GEORDIES

NO, HE'S A TREE LEAPER!

WE'RE NOT STAYING HERE TO BE INSULTED.

YOU'RE RIGHT. COME TO OUR GANG HUT SO WE CAN HAE A SEAT AND INSULT YOU IN COMFORT.

THE NEXT MORNING...

SOMEBODY'S HEARD WOR SINGIN', LADS. THEY WANT US TO ENTER THIS CONTEST.

THE DANDYVISION SINGING COMPETITION
SATURDAY AT 7 AT THE BANDSTAND IN THE PARK!

THEY WANT YOU TO ENTER BECAUSE YOU'RE SO BAD YOU'LL MAKE THEM ALL LOOK GREAT.

DON'T YOU SAY THAT ABOUT MY BONNY LADS.

SAY THAT AGAIN, YOU BIG LUMP.

I'LL SAY IT TWICE - ONCE FOR EACH OF YOUR BRAIN CELLS.

COME AWAY, BIG JOCK, HE'S NOT WORTH IT.

AT LEAST I'VE GOT THE GUTS TO SING.

WE'LL BE THERE AT THE CONTEST. DON'T YOU WORRY.

THE JOCKS WILL BE THERE. THAT MEANS WE HAVE TO BEAT THEM. WE HAVE TO BE GOOD.

HOW WILL WE DO THAT, LIKE? WE'RE A BIT RUBBISH, REALLY.

WE'LL PRACTISE. NOW, ONE, TWO, THREE...

..LAAA-LAAA!

UNCLE BERT HAS BOUGHT THE OLD COTTAGE ON THE EDGE OF TOWN!

CAN I HELP YOU, UNCLE BERT?

THAT'S KIND OF YOU, KATE. CAN YOU TAKE SOME OF THIS STUFF? I CAN'T PUT IT ON THE FLOOR AS THE BOXES WOULD GET WET.

BAH! I'M TOO SHORT TO REACH THE BOXES AT THE TOP!

HANG ON, I HAVE ANOTHER SOLUTION!

GASP! HERE, TAKE THE KEY AND OPEN THE FRONT DOOR, PLEASE!

WHAT A LOVELY OLD KEY!

I'VE ALWAYS WANTED TO PEEK THROUGH THIS KEYHOLE! OLD COTTAGES FASCINATE ME!

OOH, THERE'S A LOVELY OLD CARVED WOODEN HANDRAIL ON THE STAIRS!

GASP! YES, BUT THIS IS GETTING HEAVY, KATE!

IT NEEDS SOME WORK, THOUGH! BIT OF DAMP ON THOSE WALLS, I THINK!

YES, KATE, BUT CAN YOU PLEASE OPEN THE DOOR?!

BAH! SPOILSPORT! OKAY, I'LL OPEN THE DOOR!

OOPS! THERE'S SOMETHING ELSE I CAN TELL YOU ABOUT THIS COTTAGE, UNCLE...

...THAT OLD KEY IS SO RUSTY IT SNAPPED IN HALF!

GAH! I SHOULD HAVE KNOWN ASKING KATE FOR HELP WOULD BE BAD LOCK!

LEW STRINGER

BERYL the PERIL

BERYL! YOUR TOAST IS GOING COLD!

I'M TRYING TO DECIDE WHAT TO WEAR, MUM!

OKAY, HEADS FOR CLASSIC RED AND BLACK, TAILS FOR CASUAL RED AND YELLOW.

TEN MINUTES LATER...

THIS TOAST IS COLD.

JUST EAT IT. WE'RE GOING TO TERY MANOR, REMEMBER?

GASP! LORD AND LADY TERY'S MEGA-POSH CASTLE?! THIS IS FAR TOO CASUAL! I NEED TO CHANGE!

YOU LOOK FINE! ALSO, IT'S NOT A CASTLE.

IT'S A STATELY HOME, BUILT IN 1794.

THERE'LL BE SUITS OF ARMOUR AND DRAGONS AND WIZARDS, THOUGH, YEAH?

NO.

THEN WHY ARE WE GOING?!

BECAUSE IT'LL BE EDUCATIONAL.

ON A SATURDAY?! HOW DARE YOU!

TERY MANOR

RECEPTION

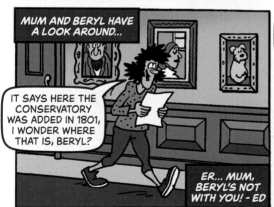MUM AND BERYL HAVE A LOOK AROUND...

IT SAYS HERE THE CONSERVATORY WAS ADDED IN 1801, I WONDER WHERE THAT IS, BERYL?

ER... MUM, BERYL'S NOT WITH YOU! - ED

HEY, MISTER! WHERE'S YOUR MOST HAUNTED BIT? I'LL SORT OUT YOUR GHOST PROBLEM.

THERE ARE NO GHOSTS HERE!

A PLACE THIS OLD? OF COURSE THERE ARE GHOSTS. I'LL SLURP THEM UP WITH MY GHOST EXTRACTOR HERE.

THAT'S A VACUUM CLEANER. OUR VACUUM CLEANER!

SOME PEOPLE DON'T WANT TO BE HELPED.

GET BACK HERE!

BERYL SEAMLESSLY BLENDS INTO A GUIDED TOUR...

EXCUSE ME! MAKE ROOM! I'M SEAMLESSLY BLENDING IN!

GUIDE

THIS IS THE LAST BOOK, HERE GOES NOTHING!

HOW TO FIND HIDDEN DOORS

BY T.C. Whatudidthere

A HIDDEN DOOR OPENS...

GET OUT OF THERE!

MEANWHILE, IN TERY MANOR'S MAIN HALL...

THAT MUST BE MISS TERY.

YOU SHOULDN'T BE BACK HERE! I DON'T EVEN KNOW WHERE 'HERE' IS!

THERE'S A DOOR UP AHEAD!

BERYL CRASHES THROUGH THE DOOR AT THE END OF THE PASSAGE...

WHOA! A WEIRD TINY ROOM WITH A DUMMY IN A CHAIR!

BERYL WAS RUNNING SO FAST, SHE FALLS OUT OF THE 'PAINTING'...

ARRGH! BERYL!

BERYL FALLS BUT CATCHES THE PIECE OF PAPER THE DUMMY OF MISS TERY WAS HOLDING...

WOW! THIS HAS A CLUE TO HIDDEN TREASURE ON IT!

IF I CAN FIGURE OUT THIS CLUE, IT'LL LEAD ME TO THE TREASURE!

WHAT'S THE CLUE?

IT SAYS, 'THE TREASURE IS HIDDEN IN THE TOWN HALL.'

WHAT DO YOU THINK IT MEANS?

REALLY?!

AT LEAST I'M THE ONLY ONE WHO KNOWS THE CLUE!

UH-OH!

HEY! THAT'S MY TREASURE!

QUICK! TO THE TOWN HALL!

THE TREASURE HUNT CONTINUES LATER IN THE ANNUAL! - ED

POSTMAN PRAT
THE WORLD'S WORST POSTIE!

KORKY THE CAT
HE'S JUST KITTEN AROUND!

OWEN GOAL
HE'S FOOTBALL CRAZY!

BRASSNECK
THE AMAZING METAL BOY!

DREADLOCK HOLMES

DREADLOCK AND HIS FAMILY ARE AT DANDYTOWN MUSEUM, WHERE DREADLOCK'S GOT A DINOSAUR FRIDGE MAGNET...

SNITCH IS ON THE TRAIL OF ANOTHER MYSTERY...

IT'S ONLY A SMALL MUSEUM, SO IT'S OKAY IF YOU WANDER OFF. WE'LL MEET BACK AT THE COFFEE SHOP.

...OR MAYBE A SAUSAGE!

OLD THINGS
GIFT SHOP
VERY OLD THINGS

WHAT'S THIS? THE HALL OF LOST THINGS?

THE HALL OF LOST THINGS

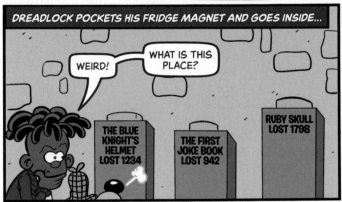

DREADLOCK POCKETS HIS FRIDGE MAGNET AND GOES INSIDE...

WEIRD!

WHAT IS THIS PLACE?

THE BLUE KNIGHT'S HELMET LOST 1234

THE FIRST JOKE BOOK LOST 942

RUBY SKULL LOST 1798

IT'S THE HALL OF LOST THINGS! DIDN'T YOU READ THE SIGN?

EVERYTHING IN HERE ISN'T IN HERE BECAUSE IT WAS LOST YEARS AGO!

WOW!

THE BLUE KNIGHT'S HELMET 1234

THIS IS THE MOST VALUABLE THING WE DON'T HAVE - THE KEY TO CACTUSVILLE!

MY MUM'S ALWAYS LOSING HER KEYS TOO!

THE KEY TO CACTUSVILLE LOST 1975

THIS IS, OR WOULD BE IF IT WASN'T LOST, MORE THAN AN ORDINARY KEY. IT'S A MAGICAL GOLDEN KEY!

COOL! I'M GOING TO FIND IT! IT'S THE CASE OF THE LOST KEY TO CACTUSVILLE!

THE KEY TO CACTUSVILLE LOST 1975

IS IT ALL RIGHT IF WE CALL IT THE KEY OF DOOM? THE LOST KEY OF DOOM SOUNDS COOLER.

NO! IF YOU FIND THE KEY, WE WON'T BE ABLE TO KEEP IT IN THE HALL OF LOST THINGS!

IT'S ALREADY NOT IN THE HALL OF LOST THINGS!

THE KEY TO CACTUSVILLE LOST 1975

YEAH, BUT, ER...

I'M FINDING IT!

AND I KNOW JUST WHO TO ASK!

THE KEY TO CACTUSVILLE LOST 1975

WHO?

IT'S ONE OF TWO PEOPLE!

THE KEY TO CACTUSVILLE LOST 1975

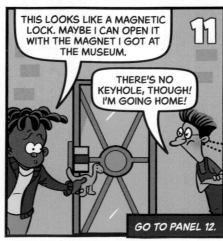

ON THE OTHER SIDE OF THE DOOR IS A VORTEX...

13

ARRGH!

GO TO PANEL 21.

THE MINE HAS A MYSTERIOUS DOOR! DO YOU KNOW HOW TO OPEN IT?

14

I FIND IF I PULL ON THE HANDLE TO ANY DOOR IT OPENS!

GO TO PANEL 15.

WHOA! A RAILROAD!

LET'S SEE WHERE IT GOES!

15

GO TO PANEL 16.

ARRGH! IT GOES DOWNHILL!

16

WHAT'S THIS? THE KEY! WE'VE FOUND IT!

GO TO PANEL 19.

17

THE TOWN HALL HAS A MYSTERIOUS DOOR! DO YOU KNOW HOW TO OPEN IT?

I FIND IF I PULL ON THE HANDLE TO ANY DOOR IT OPENS!

GO TO PANEL 18.

SHUT THAT DOOR!

18

ARRGH! IT'S THE MAYOR'S TOILET!

IT LOOKS LIKE DREADLOCK WENT WRONG SOMEWHERE! GO BACK TO THE START AND TRY AGAIN. - ED

ANOTHER DOOR AT THE END! WHERE DOES IT LEAD?

19

WE'RE GOING TO CRASH!

GO TO PANEL 22.

SHUT THAT DOOR!

20

ARRGH! IT'S THE LIGHTHOUSE KEEPER'S TOILET!

IT LOOKS LIKE DREADLOCK WENT WRONG SOMEWHERE! GO BACK TO THE START AND TRY AGAIN. - ED

YOU COULD TRY BEING A LITTLE MORE IMPRESSED BY OUR QUANTUM WORMHOLE!

21

TUT! A RESEARCH STATION ON THE MOON!

IT LOOKS LIKE DREADLOCK WENT WRONG SOMEWHERE! GO BACK TO THE START AND TRY AGAIN. - ED

I'M BACK AT THE START! THE KEY TO CACTUSVILLE OPENS THE DOOR TO CACTUSVILLE!

22

ARE YOU READY TO GO HOME YET?

GO TO PANEL 23.

I FOUND THE KEY TO CACTUSVILLE!

23

NOW YOU CAN PUT IT ON DISPLAY!

GO TO PANEL 24.

NO, I CAN'T! NOW IT ISN'T LOST! IF YOU LOSE IT AGAIN, THEN I CAN PUT IT ON DISPLAY!

24

HOW, IF YOU HAVEN'T GOT IT?

I CAN'T BECAUSE I'VE GOT IT! WHAT'S SO HARD TO UNDERSTAND?

EVERYTHING!

Winker WATSON

EARLY SUNDAY MORNING...

HURRY UP NOW, BOYS. GET ON THE SCHOOL BUS.

YAWN! WHY HAVE THEY GOT US UP SO EARLY? I WAS LOOKING FORWARD TO A LIE-IN.

WHAT'S GOING ON, SIR? WE DON'T USUALLY GO ON A SCHOOL TRIP ON A SUNDAY.

ON THE BUS, WATSON, WE NEED TO GET THERE FOR SUNRISE.

JUST BEFORE SUNRISE...

ZZZ!

DROOL!

WAKEY, WAKEY! THE EARLY BIRD GETS THE WORM. WE HAVE ARRIVED!

URRGH!

WHY ARE WE HERE? I WANT TO GO BACK TO BED.

YAWN!

QUICKLY, QUICKLY! BUT KEEP QUIET.

WHERE ARE WE ANYWAY?

LAKESIDE WALK

VISITOR CENTRE

CAR PARK

ON TODAY'S SCHOOL TRIP WE ARE TAKING YOU BOYS BIRDWATCHING.

BIRD SANCTUARY VISITOR CENTRE

WE WERE DRAGGED OUT OF BED FOR THIS? THE SUN STILL HASN'T COME UP!

THIS DOESN'T SOUND LIKE AN OFFICIAL SCHOOL TRIP.

OF COURSE IT IS! IT HAS NOTHING TO DO WITH SIGHTINGS OF THE EXTREMELY RARE GOLDEN-TAILED EAGLE AROUND HERE AND US NOT BEING ALLOWED TO LEAVE YOU BOYS UNSUPERVISED BACK AT SCHOOL!

SO...

YOU BOYS NEED A HOBBY AND BIRDWATCHING WILL BE GOOD FOR YOU. MAKE FOR THE HIDE.

GRUMBLE! I ALREADY HAVE A HOBBY, I ENJOY WATCHING THE TV!

CAN YOU IMAGINE IF WE DID SPOT THE GOLDEN-TAILED EAGLE?

BEST! DAY! EVER! THEY SAY YOUR BEST CHANCE OF SEEING ONE IS AT DAWN.

IF WE SPOT IT, WE ARE BOUND TO BE LET BACK INTO THE DANDYTOWN BIRD SPOTTERS' CLUB.

EVEN AFTER THE OSTRICH INCIDENT?

I'M SURE THEY'VE FORGOTTEN ALL ABOUT THAT.

ZZZZ!

THIS IS RIDICULOUS. I SHOULD BE BACK IN BED.

NOW WHAT?

NOW, WE SIT HERE AND WAIT.

I NEED TO *HATCH* A PLAN TO GET US OUT OF THIS.

JUST GOING TO THE VISITOR CENTRE TO USE THE TOILET, SIR.

SHHH! FINE, JUST BE QUICK.

AT THE VISITOR CENTRE...

Bird Mugs

HATS

I ♥ BIRDS!

Gift Shop

DUCK

BIRDS & MORE BIRDS

GIVE A HOOT FOR OWLS

PAY HERE

CUDDLY TOYS

BRILLIANT. THIS LOOKS LIKE THE ONE CREEPY AND THE HEAD ARE TRYING TO SPOT.

SO...

THIS IS THE PERFECT PLACE TO PERCH MY NEW FEATHERED FRIEND.

WHAT'S THAT OVER THERE, SIR? ISN'T THAT THE GOLDEN-TAILED EAGLE?

I DON'T BELIEVE IT. IT IS!

SO THAT MEANS WE CAN GO NOW, RIGHT?

YAY!

NO WAY, WE NEED TO CALL THE PRESIDENT OF THE DANDYTOWN BIRD SPOTTERS' CLUB AND GET HIM DOWN HERE.

ONE PHONE CALL LATER...

OUTSTANDING! WHAT A FIND. I'M GLAD YOU CALLED.

WOW!

SO, WE ARE BACK IN THE DANDYTOWN BIRD SPOTTERS' CLUB?

BUT...
SOMETHING ISN'T RIGHT. THAT BIRD HASN'T MOVED AT ALL.

IT'S A FAKE!

WHAT KIND OF STUNT ARE YOU TRYING TO PULL HERE?

B-BUT... I...

IT MUST HAVE BEEN ONE OF THE BOYS!

US?! BUT WE'VE BEEN SAT IN THIS BIG BIRD SHED THE WHOLE TIME.
SHAME ON YOU FOR BLAMING THIS DASTARDLY AND DISHONOURABLE STUNT ON YOUR STUDENTS!

WATCH OUT, SIRS, IT LOOKS LIKE A FLOCK OF ANGRY BIRD SPOTTERS IS STARTING TO FORM.
GRR!

IT'S TIME FOR US TO FLY!
TO THE BUS!

YOU'LL NEVER BE ALLOWED BACK INTO THE DANDYTOWN BIRD SPOTTERS' CLUB!

PHEW! I DIDN'T KNOW BIRDWATCHING COULD BE SO DANGEROUS.
HA! WE SHOULD BE BACK AT GREYTOWERS IN TIME FOR MY MID-MORNING NAP.

ALAN RYAN!

POSTMAN PRAT THE WORLD'S WORST POSTIE!

KORKY THE CAT HE'S JUST KITTEN AROUND!

OWEN GOAL HE'S FOOTBALL CRAZY!

BRASSNECK THE AMAZING METAL BOY!

PINKY'S CRACKPOT CIRCUS

NEXT...

NEXT...

ON BOARD...

HELLO, I'M JILL, I'LL BE YOUR ENTERTAINMENT MANAGER FOR THE VOYAGE.

ME! ME! ME! MISS! WILL WE BE ATTACKED BY PIRATES?

HA-HA-HA! NO.

HMPH! THAT DOESN'T SOUND VERY ENTERTAINING!

ONE GOOD GAME TO PLAY ON BOARD IS SHUFFLEBOARD.

ARRGH! LEG IT! A GAME THAT'S NOT ON A DEVICE!

CUDDLES AND DIMPLES DON'T MANAGE TO GET AWAY...

SHUFFLEBOARD IS EASY.

WITH THE PADDLE, SHOVE THE PUCK SO IT SLIDES INTO A HIGH-SCORING ZONE.

WHY DON'T YOU TRY?

THAT MAY BE A TOUCH TOO MUCH POWER.

TRY AGAIN!

CRACK!

TRY AGAIN, BUT LIKE I SAY, WITH A BIT LESS FORCE.

CRACK!

OKAY, WE'RE STOPPING THIS NOW. WE DON'T HAVE INFINITE PUCKS!

CRACK!

KATE'S NOT HAPPY...

WHAT'S THIS?!

ARE THERE NO KEYHOLES ON BOARD?!

EVERYONE IS A BIT BORED...

BOOOOOR... ING!

YEAH! WE'RE MOSTLY KIDS, WE DON'T WANT TO RELAX BY THE POOL. WE WANT EXCITEMENT! WE WANT SOMETHING TO HAPPEN!

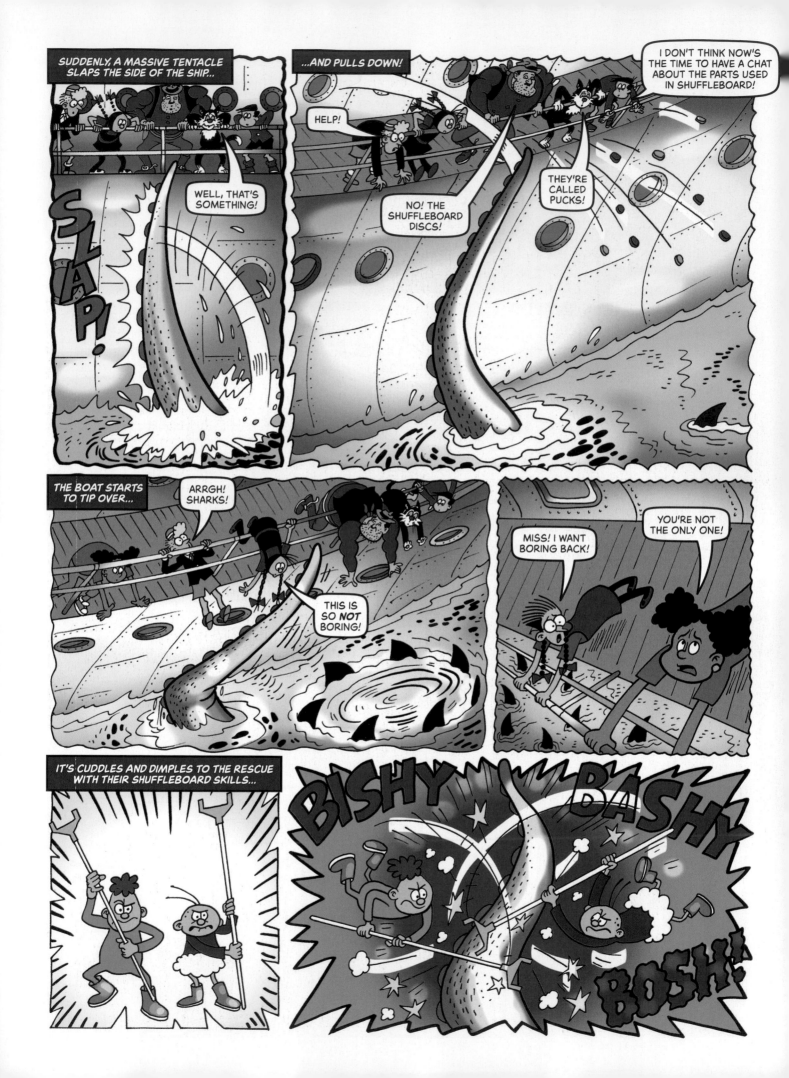

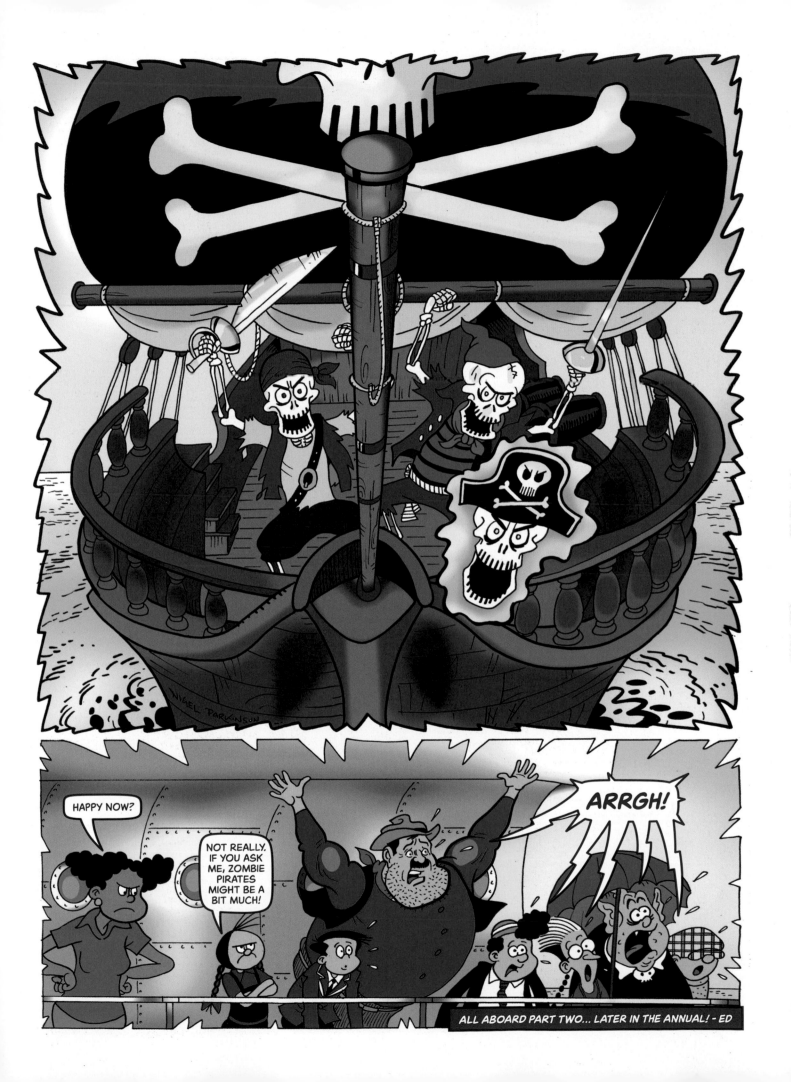

ALL ABOARD PART TWO... LATER IN THE ANNUAL! - ED

BERYL the PERIL

POSTMAN PRAT THE WORLD'S WORST POSTIE!

KORKY THE CAT HE'S JUST KITTEN AROUND!

OWEN GOAL HE'S FOOTBALL CRAZY!

BRASSNECK THE AMAZING METAL BOY!

DREADLOCK HOLMES

WINKER SCORED THE WINNING GOAL IN THE REGIONAL ALL-SCHOOLS FINAL SO HE'S VERY PROUD OF THE CUP...

GASP! THE CUP! IT'S GONE!

IT'S BEEN STOLEN! BUT BY WHO?

THIS IS A JOB FOR...

NEARBY, DREADLOCK HOLMES IS ON ANOTHER CASE...

IT'S QUIET, SNITCH. TOO QUIET!

BUT...

HONK!

WOOF! WOOF!

ALL RIGHT, SNITCH!

HONK!

NOW IT *ISN'T* QUIET ENOUGH!

HERE YOU ARE, POSTMAN PRAT, I FOUND YOUR HORN.

THANKS!

ANOTHER CASE SOLVED. I WONDER WHAT MY NEXT ONE...

DREADLOCK HOLMES, I HAVE A MYSTERY FOR YOU!

WHAT'S UP, WINKER?

THE ALL-SCHOOLS CUP HAS DISAPPEARED FROM GREYTOWERS' TROPHY CABINET!

SO...

HMM... THE CUP WAS REALLY BIG, TOO BIG TO SNEAK IT OUT OF THE SCHOOL UNNOTICED.

GASP! DO YOU THINK IT'S STILL HERE?

ARE THERE PLACES IN THE SCHOOL NO-ONE EVER GOES TO?

ER... THE ATTIC AND THE BASEMENT.

Winker WATSON

OUTSIDE THE THIRD FORM COMMON ROOM...

YAHOO! YAY!

WHAT'S GOING ON IN THERE?

WHAT DO YOU BOYS THINK YOU'RE DOING?

WE'RE WATCHING DANDYTOWN ROVERS VERSUS BEANOTOWN UNITED, SIR!

THIS PLACE IS A PIGSTY! THE TV STAYS SWITCHED OFF UNTIL THIS COMMON ROOM IS SPICK AND SPAN AGAIN!

CLICK!

WHAT ARE WE GOING TO DO, WINKER? WE'LL MISS THE SECOND HALF!

WE NEED A MATCH-WINNING WANGLE!

IT'S TIME FOR ME TO MAKE A CALL. THE CALL OF NATURE.

HUH?

THIS WEEK'S ISSUE OF 'PLANET OF ANIMALS' CAME WITH A FREE BIRD CALLER.

WHISTLE! TWEET! COO!

THESE CRISP CRUMBS WILL BE PECKED UP IN NO TIME.

IT'S WORKING.

PECK!

BUT...

HOW DO WE GET RID OF THE BIRDS, WINKER?

HOW DID THAT RHYME GO? 'THERE WAS AN OLD LADY WHO SWALLOWED A BIRD, TO CATCH A SPIDER, TO CATCH A FLY.'

Keyhole Kate

KATE AND HER DAD ARE TIDYING UP GRANDMA'S GARDEN...

MY SPADE'S HIT SOMETHING!

WHAT IS IT, DAD?

CLUNK!

IT'S SOME SORT OF TIN BOX!

IT MIGHT CONTAIN TREASURE! WE COULD BE RICH!

I COULD BUY A MANSION AND BECOME LADY KATE OF DANDYTOWN! I'D RIDE AROUND MY ESTATE ON A GOLDEN HOVERBOARD IN THE SHAPE OF A BIG KEYHOLE!

ENVY

HOW EXCITING! IF ONLY WE COULD OPEN THE BOX!

LEAVE IT TO ME, GRAN!

I'VE GOT A COLLECTION OF ANTIQUE KEYS IN MY BAG! ONE IS BOUND TO FIT!

RUMMAGE!

SIGH! ONLY MY DAUGHTER WOULD COLLECT OLD KEYS!

THIS SKELETON KEY WILL UNLOCK ANYTHING! TREASURE HERE WE COME!

CLICK!

YUCK! I'M SURE TREASURE SHOULDN'T SMELL LIKE THAT!

URRGH! WHAT COULD IT BE?

HORRID SMELL

NASTY NIFF

IT'S JUST AN OLD LUNCH BOX! THE ONLY THING INSIDE IS AN 80-YEAR-OLD CHEESE SANDWICH!

THAT STINKS!

BEST BEFORE 1942

LEW STRINGER

PINKY'S CRACKPOT CIRCUS

POSTMAN PRAT — THE WORLD'S WORST POSTIE!

KORKY THE CAT — HE'S JUST KITTEN AROUND!

OWEN GOAL — HE'S FOOTBALL CRAZY!

BRASSNECK — THE AMAZING METAL BOY!

Desperate Dan

HOP

SKIP

I'M GOING TO BE LATE FOR DINNER - I'LL CUT ACROSS THE COW FIELDS.

DON'T TRY THIS AT HOME, READERS. IT'S NOT WITHOUT ITS DANGERS. YOU'VE GOT TO BE ABLE TO DODGE THE COWPATS.

JUMP!

PHEW - NO COWPATS...

...AND NO COWS! NOT EVEN A LITTLE 'UN. WHAT'S GOING ON?

BACK HOME...

IT WAS THE STRANGEST THING, AUNT AGGIE, ALL THE COWS HAVE DISAPPEARED FROM THE FIELDS OUT YONDER.

YOU KNOW WHAT THAT MEANS?

YEP - NO MORE DODGIN' COWPATS!

TRUE, BUT ALSO...

TUCK

POSTMAN PRAT
THE WORLD'S WORST POSTIE!

I'VE BEEN GIVEN A VAN TO HELP WITH MY DELIVERIES TODAY!

THE SATNAV ISN'T WORKING, BUT THAT'S NO PROBLEM FOR ME!

I'M USING PRAT-NAV! IT'S MY INSTINCTIVE WAY OF KNOWING THE ROUTE WITHOUT ANY MAP!

OKAY, MY PRAT-NAV MIGHT BE ON THE BLINK!

LEW STRINGER

KORKY THE CAT
HE'S JUST KITTEN AROUND!

HEY - CHECK OUT THIS NEW FILTER, IT'S SO COOL!

SNAP!

I GUESS THE CAT FILTER DOESN'T WORK ON ACTUAL CATS!

OWEN GOAL
HE'S FOOTBALL CRAZY!

WE FOOTBALLERS ARE REALLY WELL LOOKED AFTER THESE DAYS. FROM MEDICAL SUPPORT...

...TO TAILORING.

THEN THERE'S THE DIETARY SPECIALISTS AND THE TACTICAL SUPPORT. IN FACT...

...WE DON'T EVEN NEED TO KICK THE BALL OURSELVES ANY MORE!

PASS TO DIMMY, PARKINSON.

AT ONCE, SIR.

BRASSNECK
THE AMAZING METAL BOY!

RATS! I WAS GOING TO PLAY MUSIC BUT MY PHONE BATTERY IS FLAT.

DON'T WORRY, I'M ON IT.

I JUST NEED THESE OLD CDS.

BUT WE'VE GOT NOTHING TO PLAY THEM ON.

DON'T WE? MMM... THESE ARE DELISH!

DJ BRASSERS IN THE HOUSE!

DIDN'T KNOW I COULD PLAY MUSIC, DID YOU?

the Jocks and the Geordies

IF I CAN FIGURE OUT THIS CLUE, IT'LL LEAD ME TO THE TREASURE!

WHAT'S THE CLUE?

IT SAYS, 'THE TREASURE IS HIDDEN IN THE TOWN HALL.'

UH-OH!

TURN ROOND! IT'S AT THA BANK!

AND NOW...

THESE ARE THE PLANS TO THE BANK.

ISN'T ROBBING A BANK ILLEGAL?

MEANWHILE...

THAT LASSIE'S LONG GONE, AND SHE DIDN'T HAVE ANY HEIRS.

AYE! HOW CAN IT BE STEALING IF IT DISNAE BELONG TO ANYONE?

HOW COME WE'RE PLANNING THIS IN FRONT OF THE JOCKS?

THE RIVAL GANGS SPLIT UP...

THE TREASURE WILL BE IN THE BASEMENT, SO A TUNNEL WILL BE OUR BEST BET TO GET IT.

AYE, THAT'S CANNY, THE JOCKS WON'T THINK OF THAT!

BUT...

THE TREASURE WILL BE IN THE BASEMENT!

AYE!

DIG! DIG! DIG!

HOW FAR IS THE BANK? THE SWEAT'S POURING OFF ME HERE!

KEEP GOING!

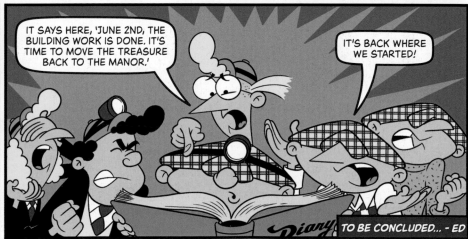

TO BE CONCLUDED... - ED

BERYL the PERIL

MATCH DAY...

DANDYTOWN UNITED FC

I CAN'T BELIEVE YOU MANAGED TO *SCORE* TICKETS TO THE BIG MATCH!

A FRIEND AT WORK SOLD ME THEM, HE HAS TO GO TO A WEDDING TODAY.

I MANAGED TO GET THEM FOR HALF THE USUAL PRICE.

RESULT!

BUT...

HERE ARE OUR TICKETS.

YIKES! THIS WILL TAKE A WHILE, FOLLOW ME.

WHAT DID HE SAY?

ONE LONG CLIMB LATER...

GRR! NOT ANY MORE.

THIS FRIEND AT WORK... CLOSE, ARE YOU?

HERE ARE YOUR SEATS, ENJOY!

I'M STARVING, CAN WE GET A BURGER?

SIGH! IT'S MILES AWAY! WAIT HERE AND SAVE OUR SEATS.

RUMBLE!

SAVE OUR SEATS? NO-ONE'S GOING TO WANT THESE SEATS.

GRUMBLE! I'LL BE BACK SOON.

UNITED

ANOTHER LONG CLIMB LATER...

PHEW! HERE YOU ARE. NOW SETTLE DOWN, THE GAME IS ABOUT TO BEGIN.

THANKS, DAD! YUM!

CHOMP!

SQUIRT!

YUCK! WHAT'S THIS?!

YOU KNOW I CAN'T STAND TOMATO SAUCE. THIS IS A *RED CARD* OFFENCE!

SO...

THE GAME'S STARTED. IF YOU WANT ANOTHER BURGER, YOU'LL HAVE TO GO THIS TIME.

FINE!

WHAT AM I SUPPOSED TO GET WITH THIS?

IT'S ALL I'VE GOT ON ME.

SHH!

ONE LONG WALK LATER...

BURGER

PUFF! PANT! ONE BURGER, PLEASE.

THAT'LL BE £5, PLEASE.

BUT ALL I HAVE IS 56 PENCE.

YOU CAN JUST ABOUT AFFORD A COUPLE OF PACKETS OF KETCHUP, IF YOU'D LIKE?

RUBBISH SEATS AND NO BURGER! I WISH I HAD A TICKET FOR THE VIP SECTION!

V.I.P BOX

STAFF ONLY

TIME FOR ME TO MAKE A QUICK *SUBSTITUTION*.

PURR-FECT!

STA ONL

SPARE

HALF-TIME...

WHAT'S TAKING THAT GIRL SO LONG?

I BET SHE'S STILL AT THE BURGER BAR. SHE'D BETTER NOT BE CAUSING ANY TROUBLE.

DRESSED LIKE THIS, I SHOULD BE ABLE TO GET MY PAWS ON LOADS OF FREE STUFF.

OFFICIAL MASCOT BUSINESS. I'LL TAKE THREE BURGERS, SOME FRIES AND TWO LARGE COLAS.

PUFF! PANT! WHERE IS SHE?

WAIT A MINUTE! I RECOGNISE THAT VOICE.

I KNEW IT!

EEK! TIME FOR ME TO GET OUT OF HERE BEFORE THERE'S A CAT-ASTROPHE!

HEY, YOU AREN'T THE MASCOT! YOU NEED TO PAY FOR ALL THIS.

THIS IS NO TIME TO LOSE MY HEAD.

WHERE DO YOU THINK YOU'RE GOING?!

ARRGH! WHERE'S THE VIP ROOM?

GET BACK HERE BEFORE YOU GET US INTO ANY MORE TROUBLE!

SOMEBODY STOP THAT MASCOT!

I THINK I MAY HAVE TAKEN A WRONG TURN.

HUH?

I'LL TAKE CARE OF THIS!

OH NO! IT'S THE BEANOTOWN UNITED MASCOT - BIFFO THE BEAR!

IN THE COMMENTARY BOX...

THE MASCOTS HAVE TAKEN OVER THE PITCH!

THEY THINK IT'S ALL OVER...

...IT IS NOW!

CRASH!

PAY UP!

PHEEP!

OFF! ALL OF YOU!

I THINK WE'D BETTER GO BEFORE IT ALL KICKS OFF!

POSTMAN PRAT
THE WORLD'S WORST POSTIE!

KORKY THE CAT
HE'S JUST KITTEN AROUND!

OWEN GOAL
HE'S FOOTBALL CRAZY!

BRASSNECK
THE AMAZING METAL BOY!

I GOT THE TOOLBOX OPEN! THINGS SHOULD GET EASIER NOW!

MR MOUSTACHE MAN, OR MIKE IF YOU WANT TO USE HIS ACTUAL NAME, IS QUITE A DEEP SLEEPER...

CRASH! BANG! BOOM! GRIND! HAMMER! BOING! SMASH! DOINK!

TING! ♪

GASP! WHAT WAS THAT?!

LYING DOWN ON THE JOB, MIKE?!

FINISHED!

I, ER...

FINISHED WHAT?

CLOTT!!!

DREADLOCK HOLMES

IT'S TEN O'CLOCK IN THE MORNING AND DREADLOCK HOLMES HAS A MYSTERY TO SOLVE...

WHY IS THE HOUSE SO DARK, MUM? IT'S ONLY TEN O'CLOCK!

IT'S THE NEW NEIGHBOURS, SHERMAN. THEY ARRIVED LAST NIGHT.

WE MAY NEVER SEE SUNLIGHT AGAIN!

DREADLOCK GOES OUTSIDE...

WHOA!

THAT'S SOME LOFT EXTENSION!

DREADLOCK DECIDES TO INVESTIGATE...

THIS MUST BE THE DOORBELL.

YOU RANG?

DID I?!

I'M DREADLOCK HOLMES, YOUR NEW NEIGHBOUR. I JUST WANTED TO INTRODUCE...

WHO'S AT THE DOOR, SHRIEK? PLEASE TELL ME IT'S A DETECTIVE!

I AM, ACTUALLY!

COME IN! THERE'S NOT A MOMENT TO LOSE!

I'M 'ERBERT HYDE. MY GREAT-GRANDFATHER LEFT ME THIS CASTLE, BUT THERE'S A MYSTERY AT ITS HEART!

IS IT HOW IT CAN MOVE DURING THE NIGHT?

NO, THAT'S JUST A THING IT DOES ONCE IN A WHILE. THE REAL MYSTERY IS...

...WHERE IS THE TOILET?

YOU DON'T KNOW WHERE THE TOILET IS?!

Winker WATSON

FORM THREE ARE ON A SCHOOL TRIP...

I WONDER WHERE CREEPY AND HEAD ARE TAKING US TODAY?

IT'S GOT TO BE MORE EXCITING THAN LAST MONTH'S TRIP TO PERKINS' PAPER CLIP FACTORY.

HERE WE ARE, BOYS!

NO WAY!

DANDYTOWN AQUARIUM!

FINALLY! A TRIP THAT ISN'T GOING TO SEND US TO SLEEP.

THE *TIDE* HAS REALLY TURNED, THIS IS TOO GOOD TO BE TRUE.

ENT

I'M GOING TO FIND THE SHARK TANK.

I WANT TO SEE THE GIANT OCTOPUS.

SLOW DOWN THERE, FORM THREE, WE ARE HERE TO WORK.

I THOUGHT THIS WAS GOING TO BE A FUN SCHOOL TRIP FOR ONCE.

WE ARE HERE TO LEARN.

FUN? WE AREN'T HERE FOR FUN.

WORK SHEETS!

OFF YOU GO, CLASS. THOSE WORKSHEETS WON'T FILL THEMSELVES!

HMM.

HA! NOW WE CAN LOOK FOR THAT BURIED TREASURE.

AND YOU'RE SURE THIS MAP IS REAL?

ABSOLUTELY. I BOUGHT THIS OFF MY FRIEND, DAVE, WHO GOT IT FROM HIS FRIEND WHO SAID THIS BELONGED TO AN EX-WORKER WHO HID SOME TREASURE IN THE AQUARIUM.

THAT'S GOOD ENOUGH FOR ME, LET'S GO.

I KNEW I SMELT SOMETHING *FISHY!*

THEY'RE HERE TO HUNT FOR SOME HIDDEN TREASURE, THEY ARE SO *SLIPPERY.*

SO...

WE NEED TO TAKE TEN PACES NORTH-WEST.

I CAN'T WAIT TO GET MY HANDS ON ALL THAT GOLD.

WE NEED TO FOLLOW THEM.

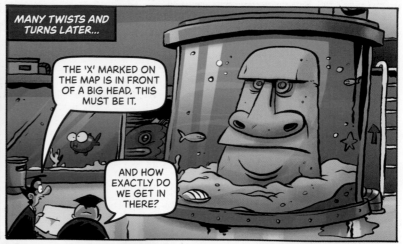

MANY TWISTS AND TURNS LATER...

THE 'X' MARKED ON THE MAP IS IN FRONT OF A BIG HEAD. THIS MUST BE IT.

AND HOW EXACTLY DO WE GET IN THERE?

WHAT WAS THAT SOUND?

I THINK WE'RE BEING FOLLOWED.

WELL, IF IT ISN'T WATSON AND TROTT.

WE KNOW ALL ABOUT YOUR TREASURE HUNT.

I'VE GOT AN IDEA ON HOW THESE TWO CAN PROVE USEFUL.

SO...

Aquarium Staff Only

YOU NEED TO PUMP AIR DOWN TO US WHILE WE DIG FOR THE TREASURE.

AND...

WHAT ARE YOU SO HAPPY ABOUT?

WE CAN LET THEM DO ALL THE DIGGING THEN SWIPE THE TREASURE FROM THEM.

BUT HOW DO WE DO THAT?

WITH THIS STINK BOMB! THE *SWEET SMELL* OF SUCCESS.

THEY'VE FLOATED UP THE TREASURE CHEST, TIME TO PUMP THE PONG!

DOWN BELOW...

COUGH! SPLUTTER! WATSON AND TROTT HAVE GONE!

THOSE ROTTERS. THEY'VE TAKEN THE CHEST. AFTER THEM!

WE NEED TO FIND SOMEWHERE QUIET SO WE CAN OPEN THIS CHEST AND SEE WHAT TREASURE'S INSIDE.

STAFF ONLY.

BUT...

EXIT

THERE'S NOWHERE TO RUN! HAND OVER THE TREASURE.

THE COMMON STARFISH CAN BE USEFUL IN THESE STICKY SITUATIONS.

Touch Pool

SPLAT!

ARRGH! GET IT OFF!

NOW FOR THE NEXT PART OF MY WANGLE - WITH THIS PEN!

MARKER

YUCK!

STOP MUCKING ABOUT AND GET THAT CHEST.

WE HAVE YOU NOW!

DETENTION FOR BOTH OF YOU FOR THE NEXT 100 YEARS. BUT FIRST, HAND OVER THE CHEST.

WATCH OUT, EVERYBODY. IT LOOKS LIKE THE AQUARIUM GLASS IS ABOUT TO CRACK!

YIKES!

ARRGH! IT COULD GO AT ANY SECOND!

HEADS AND TEACHERS FIRST!

EVERYBODY, EVACUATE THE AQUARIUM!

STAFF

SO...

THAT WANGLE WAS DRAWN TO PERFECTION!

THANKS, LET'S FIND OUT HOW MUCH TREASURE THERE IS.

MARKER

WOW! SOME OF THESE ARE OVER 70 YEARS OLD.

HA! WHAT A DANDY DISCOVERY! CREEP AND HEAD GOT SCHOOLED!

Property of Korky

DANDY

AR!

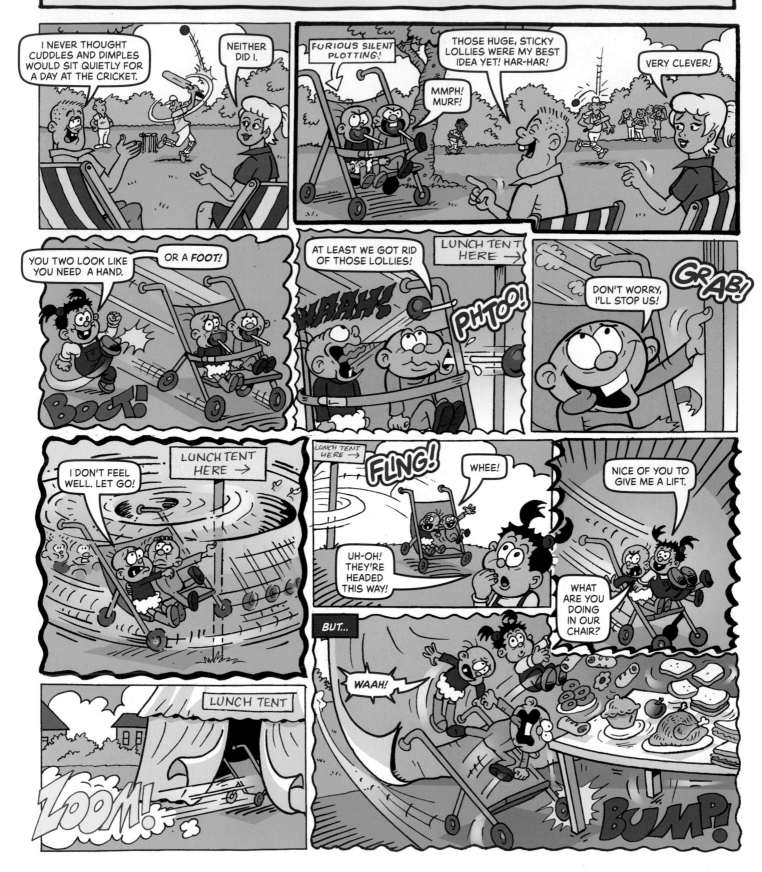

PHEW! I'VE LANDED!

THUD!

NOT QUITE, BOSS...

...THIS IS THE 'HIGH DIVE INTO A BARREL OF WATER' PART OF THE SHOW.

NICE OF YOU TO POP IN, BOSS.

WAAA...

PLUMMET!

...AAAH!

SPLADOOSH!!!

NOW YOU'VE LANDED!

SHOULD WE TURN THE HEATING ON NOW?

NO, WE WOULDN'T WANT TO UPSET PINKY.

I'M SURE HE'LL BE JUST FINE WITH A WOOLLY HAT.

IT'S F-F-FREEZING! G-G-GET ME OUT!

SHIVER!!!

SHIVER!!!

CLAP! CLAP! CLAP!

DO YOU PROMISE TO LET US GO, LIFT THE CURSE ON THE PIRATES AND GIVE YOUR DOGS SCRATCHES AND RUBS?!

YES! OKAY! OKAY!

THE GANG ROW BACK TO THE SHIP...

WE DID IT! WE WON! NOT SURE HOW, BUT WE WON!

YES! OUR TROUBLES ARE OVER!

BUT BACK ON BOARD...

ARR! THIS IS OUR SHIP NOW!

HOW UNGRATEFUL! AFTER WE GOT YOUR CURSE LIFTED!

ER, HELLO! WE'RE PIRATES!

WELL, THE CAPTAIN DID RUN OFF. WE DO SORT OF NEED A CAPTAIN.

YEAH! A CRUISE RUN BY PIRATES SOUNDS AWESOME!

YEAH!

IT'S NOT THE SAME WHEN YOU *WANT* US TO PIRATE!

GO ON! PLEASE!

OKAY! CAPTAIN NO BEARD'S PIRATE CRUISES IT IS! LET'S HAVE A PARTY!

HOORAY!!

OUR TROUBLES ARE OVER!

THE END!

POSTMAN PRAT THE WORLD'S WORST POSTIE!

THAT'S ME FINISHED FOR TWO WEEKS! NOW TO BOOK A HOLIDAY!

POST OFFICE DEPOT.

WOW! FLIGHTS ARE SO EXPENSIVE! I CAN'T AFFORD THAT!

DANDYSKIES AIRWAYS £1,000 £2,500

THE COST OF POSTAGE IS MUCH CHEAPER! I WONDER...

POST OFFICE

TO: SOMEWHERE HOT LIKE SPAIN. FIRST CLASS

NO, PRAT, YOU CANNOT POST YOURSELF ON HOLIDAY!

LEW STRINGER

KORKY THE CAT HE'S JUST KITTEN AROUND!

WAHEY! THIS IS SO MUCH FUN!

HE

OH NO - MY KITE IS STUCK. I'D BETTER TRY TO GET IT DOWN.

BUT...

I'VE GOT THE KITE, BUT HOW DO I GET DOWN?!

SO...

A CAT STUCK IN A TREE BEING RESCUED BY A FIREFIGHTER... HOW ORIGINAL!

FIRE

OWEN GOAL HE'S FOOTBALL CRAZY!

SOME PEOPLE SAY THAT FOOTBALLERS ARE A LITTLE DRAMATIC. WHAT DO YOU THINK, OWEN?

OWEN?

OWEN, CAN YOU JUST...

TAP

ARRGH! MY SHOULDER! WAAH! I THINK IT'S BROKEN!

I CAN'T IMAGINE WHERE PEOPLE GET THAT IDEA FROM!

BRASSNECK THE AMAZING METAL BOY!

I LOVE GOING TO THE BEACH WHEN IT'S SUNNY.

SO DO I.

WHAT ARE YOU DOING, BRASSNECK? YOU CAN'T GET TOO HOT, YOU'RE A ROBOT.

NO, BUT I LOVE THE SUN...

...BECAUSE IT'S GREAT FOR MY SOLAR PANELS. IT'S THE GREENEST WAY TO RECHARGE MY BATTERIES.

HEE-HEE!

BERYL the PERIL

VERY EARLY IN THE MORNING...

WAKE UP, BERYL, WE'RE HERE.

YAWN! WHERE?

I'M TAKING YOU ON A DADDY-DAUGHTER FISHING TRIP!

YOU WOKE ME UP MEGA-EARLY SO WE CAN SIT ON SOME MUDDY BANK AND STARE AT THE WATER FOR HOURS?! NO THANKS.

I HIRED US A BOAT.

WHY DIDN'T YOU SAY SO?! TAKE ME TO MY SHIP!

WHOOSH!

SO...

I CAN'T WAIT TO SEE THE BRILLIANT BOAT YOU GOT US!

HERE WE GO, BERYL. WHAT DO YOU THINK?

WOW! IT'S SO COOL!

THAT'S NOT OUR BOAT, WE'RE THE ONE NEXT TO IT.

ALL ABOARD...

HOW'S THIS WRECK STILL AFLOAT?

STOP COMPLAINING AND GET DOWN HERE, YOU CAN HELP ME CAST OFF.

FIND THE BAIT BOX FOR ME, WOULD YOU?

PHEWY! SOMETHING SMELLS FISHY.

WAFT!

CORPORAL CLOTT

PREVIOUSLY...

THIS TOAST IS COLD...

JUST EAT IT. WE'RE GOING TO TERY MANOR, REMEMBER?

IT'S A STATELY HOME, BUILT IN 1794.

THERE'LL BE SUITS OF ARMOUR AND DRAGONS AND WIZARDS, THOUGH, YEAH?

NO.

THEN WHY ARE WE GOING?!

AT TERY MANOR...

THE HOUSE IS NAMED AFTER LADY TERY WHO WAS A KEEN GARDENER. SO KEEN SHE HAD A HUGE CONSERVATORY ADDED TO THE HOUSE IN 1801.

GUIDE

LADY TERY NEVER MARRIED. SHE LOVED ONLY HER PLANTS.

GUIDE

IF I CAN FIGURE OUT THIS CLUE, IT'LL LEAD ME TO THE TREASURE!

WHAT'S THE CLUE?

IT SAYS, 'THE TREASURE IS HIDDEN IN THE TOWN HALL.'

UH-OH!

CAN I GET A BLUE LOLLY, PLEASE? DID YOU KNOW THERE'S TREASURE HIDDEN AT THE TOWN HALL? THAT'S WHERE I'M GOING NOW.

LATER, AT THE TOWN HALL..

TURN ROOND! IT'S AT THA BANK!

THEN, AT THE BANK...

IT SAYS HERE, 'JUNE 2ND, THE BUILDING WORK IS DONE. IT'S TIME TO MOVE THE TREASURE BACK TO THE MANOR.'

IT'S BACK TO WHERE WE STARTED!

AND NOW, THE EXCITING CONCLUSION...

WAS I GOING SOMEWHERE?

EXCUSE ME! CAN YOU REMEMBER WHERE I WAS GOING?

THAT'S WOR TREASURE!

BISH! BASH! BOSH!

A GEORDIE FALLS OUT...

ARE YOU OKAY? YOU LOOK TIRED!

AYE, FIGHTIN'S HARD WORK, LIKE!

THA TREASURE WASN'T AT THA TOON HALL OR THA BANK. IT'S BACK AT THA BIG HOOSE!

NOW I'M GONNA HAVE A NAP 'COS I'M WORN OOT!

BOSH!

IT WAS LUCKY I BUMPED INTO THIS FRENCH LAD! IT'S BACK TO THE HOOSE, WHICH IS FRENCH FOR HOUSE.

ZZZ!

CLOTT JOINS A TOUR AT TERY MANOR...

WHY AM I STILL HERE? THE TREASURE'S AT THE TOWN HALL!

BECAUSE I PAID FOUR QUID TO GET IN HERE!

MOVING ON...

A SLEEPY FRENCH BOY TOLD ME IT WAS BACK HERE.

GASP! THEN THAT MUST BE TRUE!

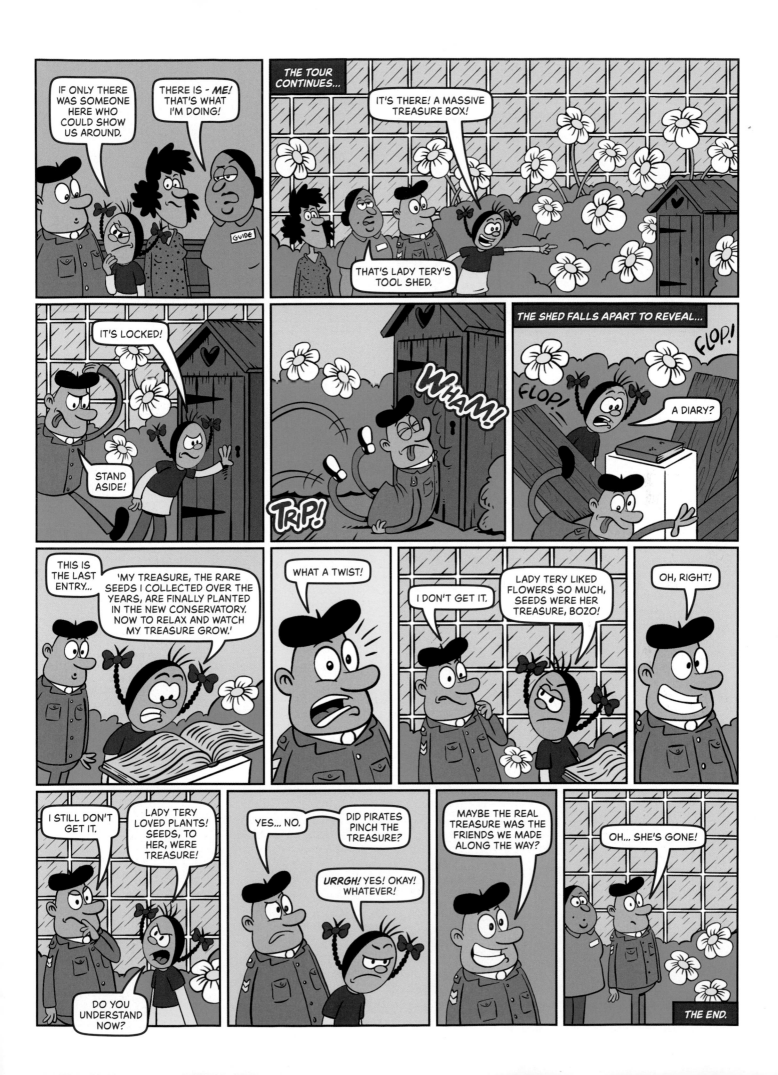

POSTMAN PRAT THE WORLD'S WORST POSTIE!

IT'S CHRISTMAS WEEK! MY FAVOURITE TIME OF YEAR!

IT'S TRADITIONAL FOR CUSTOMERS TO GIVE POSTAL WORKERS *TIPS* AT CHRISTMAS! I CAN'T WAIT! I'M GONNA BE RICH!

YOU SHOULD DELIVER OUR CHRISTMAS CARDS ON TIME!

STOP BENDING PARCELS TO SHOVE THROUGH OUR LETTERBOXES!

DON'T SEND LETTERS TO THE WRONG ADDRESS!

SIGH. NOT THE SORT OF *TIPS* I WAS EXPECTING!

LEW STRINGER

KORKY THE CAT HE'S JUST KITTEN AROUND!

TODAY, WE'RE COOKING WITH KORKY! THIS IS YOUR MAIN INGREDIENT - THE BIGGEST FISH YOU CAN GET YOUR HANDS ON.

NOW, THE SECRET IS NOT TOO LITTLE, NOT TOO MUCH.

GULP!

PERFECT!

HE

OWEN GOAL HE'S FOOTBALL CRAZY!

I'M REFEREEING A GAME TODAY - WITH THE HARDEST AND MEANEST PLAYERS EVER TO GRACE A FOOTBALL FIELD.

N.R.

THE PLAYERS ARE WILD - THEY FIGHT, ARGUE, THEIR DRIBBLING IS TERRIBLE AND DON'T EVEN THINK ABOUT GIVING ONE A RED CARD!

YUP, TODDLER FOOTBALL IS THE WORST!

DON'T PICK UP THE BALL! THAT'S AGAINST THE RULES!

PHEEP
PHEEP

WAAH!

GOO-GOO!

WUN AWAY! WUN AWAY!

BRASSNECK THE AMAZING METAL BOY!

I'D BETTER TELL MUM WE'RE RUNNING A BIT LATE, BRASSNECK.

GOOD IDEA, CHARLEY.

RATS, I'VE LEFT MY PHONE AT HOME.

NO WORRIES,

HAVE YOU GOT A MOBILE?

SOMETHING LIKE THAT...

HEE-HEE!

Winker WATSON

TODAY WE WILL BE DEDICATED TO ART.

ALL DAY, SIR?

YES, ALL DAY, WATSON.

I WANT YOU TO STUDY YOUR SUBJECT. PAY CLOSE ATTENTION TO THE LINES AND SHADOWS. BREATHE LIFE INTO YOUR WORK WITH EVERY BRUSHSTROKE.

WHAT ARE WE MEANT TO BE PAINTING, SIR?

ME!

SIGH!

AN HOUR LATER...

YAWN! THIS IS SO BORING.

ZZZZ!

OKAY, CLASS, PUT DOWN YOUR BRUSHES AND SHOW ME YOUR MASTERPIECES.

SPLUTTER! OH NO, I NEED TO PAINT SOMETHING QUICKLY.

AWFUL! TERRIBLE! THESE ARE CRIMES AGAINST ART.

WATSON, LET'S SEE WHAT YOU'VE MANAGED TO COME UP WITH.

IT'S, ER... MINIMALIST, SIR.

NICE TRY. RUBBISH IS WHAT IT IS.

SIGH! EVERYONE'S A CRITIC.

HAVE NONE OF YOU THE ARTISTIC FLAIR NEEDED TO BECOME AN ARTIST?!

chuck

WANT MORE...
PUZZLES
COMICS
JOKES
PRANKS
PRIZES
...EVERY WEEK?
YULE LOVE IT!
WE MAKE IT REIN LAUGHS!
HAVE YOUR ELF A MENACING LITTLE CHRISTMAS WITH BEANO EVERY WEEK!
BE BORED SNOW MORE WITH...
BEANO.COM
BEANO
ON SALE EVERY WEDNESDAY!

Pinky's Crackpot Circus

CUDDLES AND DIMPLES

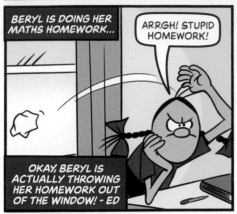

BERYL IS DOING HER MATHS HOMEWORK...

ARRGH! STUPID HOMEWORK!

OKAY, BERYL IS ACTUALLY THROWING HER HOMEWORK OUT OF THE WINDOW! - ED

OOPS!

I SUPPOSE I'D BETTER GET THAT BACK!

SOME OLD FELLA'S PICKED IT UP!

SUDDENLY...

SCREECH!

WE'LL HAVE THAT!

WHAT?!

THAT WAS WEIRD!

THIS IS A CASE FOR DESPERATE DAN!

WHAT?! - ED

ER... I MEAN DREADLOCK HOLMES!

PHEW! - ED

SOON, AT DREADLOCK'S HOUSE...

...THEN THE VAN SPED OFF ONE WAY AND THE OLD FELLA WENT THE OTHER!

SO, CAN YOU FIND MY MATHS HOMEWORK? I NEED IT FOR TOMORROW!

YES...

...AFTER MY TEA.

WOULD YOU LIKE SOME, BERYL? I MADE EXTRA.

LATER, AT THE SCENE OF THE CRIME...

THE OLD GUY WENT THIS WAY?

YES, AND THE VAN WENT THAT WAY.

1

TO FOLLOW THE OLD FELLA, GO TO PANEL 2.
TO FOLLOW THE VAN, GO TO PANEL 3.

the Jocks & the Geordies in "Posh Boys"

CRUNCH!

ARRGH!

THE ROTTEN SCUNNERS DIDNAE TOUCH THE WALLS — BUT THEY BOOBY-TRAPPED THE FLOOR!

THIS WASN'T US, MAN, BUT IT'S WHAT YE GET FOR WRECKIN' OUR HUT.

BUT WE DIDNAE.

DO YOU BELIEVE THEM?

WELL, WE DIDN'T TOUCH THEIR HUT.

SCOOSH THEM, LADS!

GLUB!

HAVING TROUBLE WITH YOUR FEET, LADS?

THAT WAS LIQUID SOAP, IN CASE YOU DIRTY RATS HAVE NEVER SEEN IT — AN' THIS IS WATER.

URRGH!

ARRGH! IT'S REALLY SLIPPERY!

I WAS GOING TO SAY THAT, MAN!

CRUMP!

AN' THAT'S WHAT YOU GET FOR MESSIN' WITH OUR HUT.

WE DIDN'T TOUCH IT, MAN.

BUT I'LL TOUCH YOU WITH A RIGHT HOOK.

IN YOUR DREAMS.